THE GREAT BOOK OF ANIMAL KNOWLEDGE

REINDEER

Crowned Deer of the North Pole

All Rights Reserved. All written content in this book may NOT be reproduced in any form or by any means, including scanning, photocopying, or otherwise without prior written permission of the copyright holder. Copyright © 2014

Some Rights Reserved. All photographs contained in this book are under the Creative Commons license and can be copied and redistributed in any medium or format for any purpose, even commercially. However, you must give appropriate credit, provide a link to the license, and indicate if changes were made.

Introduction

Photo by Andrew E. Russell (flickr.com/25949441@N02), as licensed under CC BY 2.0 Generic

We all know who Santa is, what he does, and what he rides. And today we're going to learn about his faithful reindeer! Reindeer can't actually fly like in the stories, but they are actually used by people to carry heavy loads. They are sturdy, strong animals that can survive extremely cold temperatures. Let's learn more about this amazing animal!

What Reindeer Look Like

Photo by Robin McConnell (flickr.com/robinmcconnell), as licensed under CC BY 2.0 Generic

Reindeer are large, stocky deer with large antlers that look like a branch with twigs. They have shorter legs compared to other deer. Reindeer are colored different shades of brown, and sometimes even almost white. They also have furry hooves and a nose that is covered with hair. There are actually some reindeer with red noses like Rudolph! These are very rare though, most reindeer have black noses.

Size and Weight

The size and weight of reindeer varies between subspecies. Reindeer can grow up to 6.6 ft (2 m) from head to the base of their tail. And their height can reach up to 4.9 ft (1.5 m). Average reindeer weigh around 400 pounds (180 kg).

Where Reindeer Live

Reindeer live in cold, cold places. They live nearby and inside the Arctic Circle! They are found in the tundra and woodlands of Canada, Russia, Scandinavia, Greenland, and Alaska. Reindeer are well adapted to survive the extreme cold temperatures where they live.

Fur

Photo by Eric Kilby (flickr.com/ekilby), as licensed under CC BY-SA 2.0 Generic

In order to survive the cold, reindeer need a good coat to keep warm. Their fur is perfect for keeping them warm. They have two layers of fur, a short, soft undercoat and long guard hairs. The guard hairs are hollow, and the air trapped inside the guard hairs help keep the reindeer warm. The hollow guard hairs also allow reindeer to float when swimming.

Hooves

Photo by Adrián Pérez (flickr.com/aperezdc), as licensed under CC BY-SA 2.0 Generic

Reindeer have very interesting and unique hooves. After winter, when the snow melts and the ground is wet, the foot pads of reindeer become sponge-like. This helps them walk in the wet ground. During winter, the hooves of reindeer harden, allowing them to dig on the ice and snow and to walk on slippery surfaces. Reindeer also have dewclaws, a false hoof formed by their side toes that help them walk on rocky terrains.

Antlers

Antlers are the crown of a reindeer. Their huge, beautiful antlers can grow over 4 ft (1.2 m) long! Reindeer are the only type of deer that both male and females grow antlers. Males use their antlers for fighting each other, and it is believed that the female's antlers help attract a mate. Antlers are also used for fighting off predators and digging in the snow. The antlers of reindeer shed and grow back every year. This is known as the antler cycle.

Velvet

Unlike horns, the antlers of reindeer need blood and nutrients to grow. This is what velvet is for. When the antlers are growing, it is covered in short fuzzy fur which supplies the antlers with its needs. When the antler is fully grown, the velvet falls off. Reindeer rub their antlers on trees and hard surfaces to remove the velvet.

Nose

Reindeer are the only species of deer that has a nose that is fully covered in fur. Their nose is specially designed to help them survive the cold. When cold air passes through their nostrils, it warms the air first before it reaches their lungs. Reindeer's sense of smell is also strong. They can smell food under the snow and they can also smell predators coming.

What Reindeer Eat

Photo by Madeleine Deaton (flickr.com/madeleine_h), as licensed under CC BY 2.0 Generic

Reindeer are herbivores, which means that they eat plants and plant material. Reindeer enjoy eating leaves, herbs, ferns, and mosses. Their favorite leaves are the leaves of birch and willow trees. During winter, when there is less food, reindeer use their hooves to dig up the snow to eat the lichen (also called reindeer moss) and fungi on the ground.

Stomach

Like cows, goats, and some other animals, reindeer can bring up the food in their stomach back to their mouth and chew it again. Their stomach also has a special enzyme that can break down lichen. Lichen is tough to break down, but the reindeer stomach can handle it.

Groups

Reindeer live in groups of 10 to hundreds of individuals. These groups are called herds. Living in large groups makes the reindeer safer from predators. They also like to travel together in search of food. Sometimes, extremely large groups of up to 500,000 reindeer are formed!

Breeding

The reindeer breeding season occurs during late September to early November. During this time, males fight each other for the right to mate a harem of females. They fight with their horns, and sometimes the loser dies. Males lose a lot of body weight during this time. They have to use lots of energy to fight and they are busy during this time, they don't have much time to eat.

Baby Reindeer

Female reindeer are pregnant for about 7 months. They usually give birth to only one calf at a time, though there are sometimes twins, and on rare occasions 3-4 babies. Baby reindeer are able to stand just 1 hour after birth! They can walk and follow their mother after a few more hours. Reindeer calves drink their mother's milk, but after only one week they start eating solid foods. Reindeer grow quickly, and after a few weeks with only their mother they will go to join a herd.

Migration

Photo by Bering Land Bridge (flickr.com/bering_land_bridge), as licensed under CC BY 2.0 Generic

Reindeer herds can travel long, long distances in search of food. In fact, they are the farthest traveling land animal in the world! When summer is near, large groups of reindeer migrate north to the places with plenty food. When winter is approaching, reindeer start moving southward to escape the cold. Scientists say that reindeer travel about 3000 miles (4800 km) every year!

Movement

Photo by Kitty Terwolbeck (flickr.com/kittysfotos), as licensed under CC BY 2.0 Generic

Reindeer can run at speeds up to 50 miles (65 km) an hour. They are also good swimmers. Their hooves, which are broad and flat, are great for pushing aside the water and swimming. Also, as said before, the guard hairs of reindeer are hollow, this allows them to float easily.

Predators

Reindeer are definitely not an easy animal to kill. They are big, have scary antlers, and live in groups. However, in the arctic, food is scarce sometimes, and hunting a reindeer may be worth the risk. Wolves hunt reindeer in packs, and sometimes brown bears and polar bears attack adults. Young reindeer are the most vulnerable. Aside from wolves and bears, they have to worry about eagles, foxes, lynxes, coyotes, and mountain lions.

Humans and Reindeer

Reindeer have been domesticated by humans since a long time ago; more than a thousand years! Reindeer are still the only species of deer to be widely domesticated. In some places, people use the reindeer to carry heavy loads through the snow. They also farm them for their meat, skin, and bones. Reindeer are a main food source for some tribes. Other parts of the reindeer are also used to make clothes, shelter, and tools.

Caribous

Some people are confused, what is the difference between reindeer and caribous? There is no difference. Reindeer and Caribous are the same species rangifer tarandus. In Europe, they are known as reindeer. Wild rangifer tarandus in North America are called caribous. However, domesticated populations in North America are called reindeer.

Relatives

Reindeer are part of the deer family. There are two subfamilies in the deer family, old world deer and new world deer. Reindeer are part of the new world deer subfamily with moose and elks.

Threats

Photo by peupleloup (flickr.com/peupleloup), as licensed under CC BY-SA 2.0 Generic

Reindeer's conservation status is listed as 'least concern', meaning that there are still lots of reindeer in the world and their population is stable. Hunting reindeer purely for sport is illegal. However, global warming may become a serious threat to reindeer soon.

For more information about our books, discounts and updates, please Like us on FaceBook!

Facebook.com/GazelleCB

Made in the USA
Middletown, DE
09 December 2021